Pangolin Patterns

Printed in the United States of America

First Printing, 2023

ISBN 9798390888735

EcoMavenLabs

www.ecomavenlabs.com

Table of Contents

Illustrations

Contents

Bonus Content

Introducing the Pangolin

Pangolins are amazing animals that are covered in scales and live in Africa and Asia. They get their name from 'penggulung,' the Malay word for roller, because of their adorable defense mechanism of rolling into a ball. They are the only mammals in the world that are completely covered in scales, which make them look like walking pine cones or artichokes! There are eight different species of pangolins, and they all have unique features that make them special. In this book, we will get to know all eight variations and what makes them each special.

Unfortunately, pangolins are in danger because people hunt them for their scales and meat. Each year, a staggering number of pangolins are poached from the wild across Africa and Asia. In some cultures, they are even believed to have mystical or magical properties, furthering the risk to this unique creature. This is a big problem because pangolins are very important to their ecosystems. They help control the populations of insects, and their burrows provide homes for other animals.

Don't worry though, there are things we can do to help this species that has existed for an estimated 80 million years. By learning about them and spreading the word, we can help protect these amazing animals and ensure that they continue to thrive in the wild.

A Mountain Expedition

The Diverse Pangolin Species

There are eight different species of pangolins, each with their own unique features. Four live in Asia, and four are natives of Africa.

Black-bellied pangolins are small and live in forests and grasslands. They have black scales on their bellies and tails, which helps them blend in with their surroundings.

White-bellied pangolins are larger than Black-bellied pangolins and have white scales on their bellies and tails. They live in forests and savannas.

Giant Ground pangolins are the largest of all the pangolin species and can grow up to 6 feet long! They live in forests and savannas and have a special defense mechanism: they can roll up into a ball to protect themselves from predators.

Temminck's Ground pangolins are smaller and live in forests and grasslands. They have very long tails, which help them balance as they climb trees and walk on the ground.

Each species of pangolin has its own unique features and characteristics, and all of them are important to their ecosystems. They all have long claws and surprisingly, they are really great swimmers.

Walking Along A Sandy Beach

Pangolin Anatomy

Pangolins have a distinctive anatomy that makes them well-suited to their way of life. Their most recognizable feature is their scales, which protect them from predators and insects. The scales make up 20% of their body weight, are made of keratin (the same material that makes up human hair and nails). Their overlapping scales create a flexible armor that they can curl up into to defend themselves.

The long, sticky tongue combined with their saliva helps them catch ants and termites, the mainstay of their diet. A pangolin tongue can be longer than the rest of their entire bodies. Up to 28 inches! They also have no teeth and they rely on their stomachs to grind up the insects they consume. They have powerful muscles in their stomachs that break down the tough exoskeletons of ants and termites.

Although pangolins have poor eyesight, they have excellent hearing and a keen sense of smell, which helps them locate their prey. In addition to digging for their food, they use their strong claws to climb trees and walk on the ground, while their long tails help them balance.

Pangolins are also impressive swimmers and can hold their breath for several minutes while underwater! They use this skill to cross rivers and streams in search of food.

The Pangolin Diet

Pangolins' unique diet is one of the many fascinating things about these amazing creatures. Unlike other animals that are either carnivores or herbivores, pangolins are insectivores. This means they primarily feed on insects, and their diet consists mainly of ants and termites. Pangolins have a natural talent for digging, and they use their long, sharp claws to dig into ant mounds and termite nests.

Once they have located their prey, pangolins use their long, sticky tongue to capture the insects, which they then swallow whole. They can consume up to 70 million ants and termites in a single year, making them a vital part of the ecosystem. While their diet may seem unusual, it actually plays an important role in maintaining balance in the environment.

By feeding on ants and termites, pangolins help to control their populations, which can be beneficial for farmers and gardeners. In some regions, pangolins are even considered to be natural pest controllers.

However, the impact of habitat loss and hunting on pangolin populations means that it's more important than ever to protect these amazing creatures.

Grabbing A Midnight Snack

Mythology:
Legends and Folktales

Throughout history, pangolins have been a symbol of various cultural and spiritual beliefs. As we continue to learn more about these fascinating animals, we can appreciate the role they play in traditions and storytelling.

In African folklore, the pangolin is considered a powerful totem animal, believed to possess magical powers and supernatural abilities. Some cultures believe that wearing a pangolin scale or carrying a pangolin claw brings good luck and protection.

In China, pangolins are highly regarded and have been associated with wealth, prosperity, and longevity for centuries. In Chinese medicine, pangolin scales are believed to have healing properties and are used to treat a variety of ailments, from fever to arthritis.

The Native American Hopi tribe has a story about a pangolin who teaches a man how to create armor from his scales. The armor protects the man from harm, and the pangolin becomes a respected and honored animal in the tribe.

In Indonesian folklore, the pangolin is believed to possess magical powers and is often associated with the underworld. In some legends, the pangolin is a shape-shifting creature that can transform into a human or an animal.

Eat Like An Anteater, If You Can

As insectivores, pangolins eat a variety of insects, but their favorites are ants and termites. Pangolins have long, sticky tongues that they use to lap up these tiny creatures from their nests. It's quite the sight to see!

Because they can rely on either type of food source, they are considered both "myrmecophagous" and "termitophagous". But despite their insatiable appetites, pangolins are not always able to find enough food. Ants and termites can be hard to come by, especially in areas where their habitats are threatened.

That's why it's important to protect the habitats of ants and termites. By preserving the ecosystems where these insects live, we can ensure that pangolins have enough food to eat. It's also important to avoid using pesticides and other harmful chemicals that can kill off the insects that pangolins rely on. In 2016, all eight extant species of Pangolins were re-classified from Appendix II to Appendix I, the highest protection available under CITES.

Pangolins are fascinating creatures, and their unique diet is just one of the many things that makes them so special. By learning more about pangolins and their eating habits, we can better understand the important role they play in their ecosystems, and work to protect them for generations to come.

A Rainforest Adventure

Tiny and Adorable Babies

Pangolin babies - or pangopups(!!) - are minuscule, weighing only a few ounces at birth. They are also incredibly adorable with their soft scales and big eyes. These tiny creatures rely heavily on their mothers for survival during their first few months of life. In fact, pangopups will cling to their mothers' tails and ride on their backs until they are old enough to fend for themselves.

As they grow, the soft scales on their bodies harden and begin to develop into the armor-like scales that pangolins are famous for. Pangopups are born with their eyes closed and will remain with their mothers for several months until they are strong enough to venture out on their own.

While they are still young, pangolin mothers are incredibly protective of their babies. They will curl up around their young, forming a ball with their tough scales to protect them from predators. As they mature, pangopups will learn how to use their own scales to protect themselves, rolling up into a tight ball when threatened.

While pangopups do sound adorable, don't get it confused - pangolins make for terrible pets! Their desire to constantly burrow will mean you can kiss your gardens goodbye. Pangolin scales also hold no known medicinal properties, despite being hunted for them.

Danger Lurks Everywhere

Unfortunately, pangolins are facing a lot of danger and threats from predators. These predators include large cats like lions, hyenas...and humans. Sadly, humans pose the biggest threat to pangolins. These animals are hunted for their meat and scales, and are considered a delicacy in some parts of the world. The scales are also believed to have medicinal properties, which is completely untrue.

The demand for pangolin scales has caused an increase in illegal poaching, making them one of the most trafficked mammals in the world.

Pangolins are slow-moving animals that have very few defenses against predators. They can curl up into a ball when threatened, but unfortunately, this defense mechanism doesn't always work against larger predators. Pangolins rely on their camouflage to blend into their surroundings, making it harder for predators to find them, but these passive defenses don't do much against speed and human technologies.

We must work together to protect pangolins from harm and ensure their survival. It's important to educate people about the dangers of poaching and the importance of protecting their habitats. Governments and conservation organizations must take action soon to protect pangolins and their habitats to prevent their extinction.

The Arctic Explorer

Conservation:
Saving Our Scaly Friends

One of the biggest threats to pangolins is habitat loss, as their forest and grassland homes are destroyed for logging, agriculture, and development. This destruction of their habitats leaves them with nowhere to live and breed, putting their survival at risk.

There are many efforts underway to protect pangolins and their habitats. Conservation organizations are working to educate the public about the importance of pangolins and their role in the ecosystem. They are also working with governments to enforce laws against poaching and trafficking, despite a pernicious poaching industry that deals in huge amounts of trafficked pangolins every year.

Individuals can also make a difference by supporting conservation efforts and advocating for pangolin protection. This can be done by donating to organizations that work to protect pangolins, signing petitions, and spreading awareness about the issues facing pangolins.

By coming together to protect pangolins and their habitats, we can ensure that these fascinating creatures will continue to thrive in the wild for years to come. We owe it to ourselves and future generations to do everything we can to preserve these unique and valuable animals.

Raise Your Voice For Endangered Animals!

The illegal wildlife trade is a multi-billion dollar industry, and pangolins are among the most vulnerable animals on earth. Their unique appearance and supposed medicinal properties have made them highly sought after, leading to rampant poaching and trafficking. This has resulted in a drastic decline in pangolin populations, with some species on the brink of extinction.

But pangolins are not the only vulnerable targets. Many other species are also at risk due to habitat destruction, climate change, and other human activities. It's up to all of us to take action to protect these animals and their habitats.

One way to get involved is to visit **ecomavenlabs.com**, a website dedicated to raising awareness about the threats facing vulnerable species and the importance of conservation efforts.

By taking action to protect vulnerable species and their habitats, we can ensure that these amazing animals will continue to thrive for generations to come. So let's join together and make a difference!

Meet the Asian Pangolins

Chinese pangolin (Manis pentadactyla) - found in northern India, Nepal, Bhutan, Bangladesh, Myanmar, Thailand, Laos, Vietnam, and China.

Sunda pangolin (Manis javanica) - found in Southeast Asia, including Thailand, Malaysia, Singapore, Indonesia, and the Philippines.

Indian pangolin (Manis crassicaudata) - found in the Indian subcontinent, including India, Sri Lanka, Nepal, and Bangladesh.

Philippine pangolin (Manis culionensis) - found only in the Palawan Province of the Philippines.

Chinese Pangolin

Sunda Pangolin

Indian Pangolin

Philippine Pangolin

The Four Asian Pangolins

Sunda Pangolin

Chinese Pangolin

Indian Pangolin

Philippine Pangolin

Meet the African Pangolins

Cape or Temminck's pangolin (Smutsia temminckii) - found in southern and eastern Africa, including South Africa, Namibia, Botswana, Zimbabwe, Mozambique, Zambia, Malawi, Tanzania, and Kenya.

White-bellied or tree pangolin (Phataginus tricuspis) - found in West and Central Africa, including Senegal, Guinea, Sierra Leone, Liberia, Cote d'Ivoire, Ghana, Togo, Benin, Nigeria, Cameroon, Gabon, Equatorial Guinea, and Congo.

Giant ground pangolin (Smutsia gigantea) - found in West and Central Africa, including Senegal, Gambia, Guinea-Bissau, Guinea, Sierra Leone, Liberia, Cote d'Ivoire, Ghana, Togo, Benin, Nigeria, Cameroon, Central African Republic, and Congo.

Black-bellied or long-tailed pangolin (Phataginus tetradactyla) - found in West and Central Africa, including Sierra Leone, Liberia, Cote d'Ivoire, Ghana, Togo, Benin, Nigeria, Cameroon, Equatorial Guinea, and Congo.

Temmenick's Ground Pangolin

White-Bellied Pangolin

Giant Ground Pangolin

Black-Bellied Pangolin

The Four African Pangolins

White-Bellied Pangolin

Black-Bellied Pangolin

Giant Ground Pangolin

Temmenick's Ground Pangolin

Pangolin Pop Quiz!

Were you paying attention? See if you can answer the following questions.

1 What do pangolins primarily eat?

____

____

2 What is a baby pangolin called?

____

____

3 What is the unique defense mechanism of pangolins?

____

____

4 How do pangolins catch their prey?

____

____

5 Which continent has four out of the eight pangolin species?

____

____

6 How do pangolins cross rivers and streams?

____

THANKS
for reading

Answer Key

Pangolin Pop Quiz!

Were you paying attention? See if you can answer the following questions.

1 What do pangolins primarily eat?
Pangolins primarily eat insects, especially ants and termites.

2 What is a baby pangolin called?
A baby pangolin is called a pangopup.

3 What is the unique defense mechanism of pangolins?
The unique defense mechanism of pangolins is that they can roll up into a tight ball to protect themselves from predators.

4 How do pangolins catch their prey?
Pangolins catch their prey by using their long tongues and sticky saliva to capture ants and termites.

5 Which continent has four out of the eight pangolin species?
Africa has four out of the eight pangolin species.

6 How do pangolins cross rivers and streams?
Pangolins cross rivers and streams by being good swimmers and holding their breath for several minutes while underwater.

DEDICATION

For Drewasaurus
from Lisasaurus

My life started when I met you.